T0328508

LITANY OF A FOREIGN WIFE

Litany of a Foreign Wife

Poems

Nnane Ntube

Spears Media Press
Denver, Colorado

Spears Media Press LLC
Denver
7830 W. Alameda Ave, Suite 103-247 Denver, CO 80226
United States of America

First Published in 2020 by Spears Media Press
www.spearsmedia.com
info@spearsmedia.com
Information on this title: www.spearsmedia.com/litany-of-a-foreign-wife

ISBN: 9781942876564 (Paperback)

Also available in Kindle (eBook)

Cover art: Bright Toh
Cover design: Doh Kambem
Text design and typesetting by Spears Media Press LLC, Denver, CO

Dedicated to you whose voice is lost in the wind.

Contents

FOREWORD

Contemporary Anglophone Cameroon poetry has been influenced and is still being influenced by the Anglophone Cameroon socio-political context. This new wind of change now serves as a muse to budding poets whose committed pens have changed from painting the lacuna between African and Western cultures epitomized by neo-colonialists to drawing images that portray why we are so rich, yet so poor. This explains why the Anglophone Cameroon problem that broke out in late 2016 has given birth to a huge digit of angry writers of all genres of literature, particularly poetry. By this token, Anglophone Cameroon literature is becoming more committed and is growing by leaps and bounds. The poetic contribution, especially by aspiring poets has been spontaneous, evidenced by the myriad of publications seen on social media. This is a clear indication that as far as nationhood is concerned, poets too have a say to the construction of the Anglophone identity. Fortunately, or unfortunately, the only weapon these committed poets use is the pen! The pen now has become the poet's gun through which the burning Anglophone flame is being extinguished.

Chinua Achebe once said something to the effect that no country has ever handed its government to writers. It was not so much a statement about the administrative capabilities or lack thereof, of writers in government, as of the true significance of creative imagination in the shaping of human destiny at a point in time. 'The Pen,' they say, 'is mightier than the sword'. But whereas soldiers and armed forces overthrow civilian governments and impose dictatorships and totalitarian regimes across the globe, no association of writers by whatever name has ever carried out a coup d'état to topple a country's leadership.

Nnane Ntube is an aspiring Anglophone poet to watch. With her ear on the ground, her maiden collection of poems paints a portrait of a stagnating nation overwhelmed by greed, corruption, egoism and civil feud. Treading on terrain where angels fear to tread, Ntube is courageous enough to handle such vexing notions like marginalization, police brutality, cultural difference, man's inhumanity to man and the question of identity.

Litany of a Foreign Wife is unique and this makes classification easy. Nnane Ntube has a unique way of packaging her poetry that sets them apart from all other collections. Her collection of poems ranges from themes that include Cameroon, Africa and the rest of the world. The poems transcend the ordinary recitation of poems to a kind of story-telling about real human sufferings, the follies of mankind and their callous attitudes towards one another. This is because most of the poems seem to have been inspired by painful real-life experiences before and during the Anglophone Cameroon crises. For instance, the wiggled nature of her diverse thematic consideration, the notion of '*The Other*', separateness, asunder, apartness (or if you like, apartheid), tend to dominate her creative vision. Inspired by anguish and the lamentation of victims of the perennial cultural conflict in her country, Ntube raises her voice in "Hear My Broken Voice" by complaining why they always see a '*they*' in her. This is a call for re-instance that manifests itself in "Not Just News" in which she feels that marginalization and oppression have attained unquestionable heights. In desperation as she ridicules these human vices, the persona in her poem invokes retributive justice on the perpetrators of suppression as seen in "The Baptism of Fire." Here and in "The Chamber", she condemns neo-colonial idiosyncrasy for being responsible for the wanton cruelty and exploitation of their natural resources. In "Wolves", the poet-critic describes these exploiters in more concrete bitter terms, for not only their basic necessities have been snatched from them but their cherished culture. Disillusioned and frustrated, the poet exclaims, 'I'm fed up!' in "The Ice Breaker" for even love has been captured. Despite the pains, the voice in the poem "War is Shit", euphemistically and with subtleties discusses the antipathetic effects of war.

The tendency to rebel is equally very prominent in Ntube's poetry as seen in the conscientisation poem "Wake Up", and in "A Woman's Torrent". Similarly, in "A Rainy Voice" and in "Pestiferous You", she unequivocally calls for defiance with the same locution as we saw in the opening poem. To the bard, passive acceptance or submission can never free those in chains.

The notion of agitation, alienation, escape, refuge, divorce and separation are carefully wiggled in "Return-Not Going Further". Ironically, it is in this same poem that the mood of nostalgia is notorious. Here the idea of returning to the roots of the culture and tradition becomes unquestionable. Dated *1 July 2018* at *7:14 a.m.*, one is tempted to think that this verse was freely inspired by the Anglophone Cameroon crisis. Other poems in the collection also portray symbolic dates, logically linked to the uprising. For example, "Ashes", dated Yaounde, 31 January 2018; and "Awed by Silence", dated *12 February 2018* and "Life-Blood (The Message)", dated *August 2017*. These dates are suggestive of events that occurred as the Anglophone Cameroon crisis rages on.

Closely linked to alienation is homelessness which is described in "Where Shall My Abode Be?" especially as the persona finds herself in a deserted land. Gripped with this unhinging doom, the poet persona turns prophet in "The Fall of the Baobab (In Memory of Morgan Tsvangirai)" and predicts judgment for the evil perpetrators that will come only with *Time*. As a poet-psychiatrist, she diagnoses madness as an epidemic ailing the military epitomized by *dogs* in "Dogs Are Mad Again" probably judged by the atrocities they perpetuate. Following the state of shameless moral depravity and indecency publicly displayed by the young and the old, our acerbic bard sustains this motif with vent categorically in "We're All Mad".

The poet further calls out those who have taken education hostage. So, in "Life-Blood (The Message)", she describes the fact that nursery rhymes can no longer be heard, the lack of freedom of expression and inhuman prison conditions and torture in "A Hint to My Brother". Like Denis Brutus in "The Sounds Begin Again", she evokes psychological torture in most of her poems especially "The Knock (The Sound That Kills Many)" and bemoans the infectious effect of silence in "Silence" and in "Hungary Voices (The Silent Prayer)".

Despite the characteristic mood of pessimism coupled with the tone of bitterness, Nnane Ntube still feels that poetry can be used as a tool for social and political change. This explains why she describes dialogue in "Cinch" and in the title poem, *The Litany of a Foreign Wife*. Ironically, it is this central poem that conveys all the irreconcilable opposites of marginalization, conflict, love, peace, reconciliation, etc. and ends up suggesting meaningful dialogue as a path to togetherness. Though very satirical, "Yet Another Song" and "Dance Now to Dance No More" are distinguished poems in her collection that ridicule politicians who are reluctant to change.

Despite this pessimistic atmosphere that what one hopes for will not happen, glimpses of hope and optimism are deported in the last of the pivotal poem:

My husband treats me fairly
Drop your hate speeches in the dust bin
And reflect on how our future shall be,
I'll be glad to have you back
If only you give me my rightful place
And let me savour my own beauty.
Then, I'll humbly be your African pearl.

Like Geoffrey Chaucer in *The Canterbury Tales*, Nnane Ntube criticizes to correct.

By every indication, Nnane Ntube is a budding Anglophone Cameroon poet whose message should be watched keenly as it attains a universal appeal. Her simple style - free verse and lyrical prose demystifies poetry and makes it enjoyable even to young readers. What makes her poetry aesthetically profound is her unique combination of the story-telling technique with rhetoric, personification, and literary allusions in transporting her message. The feelings, the emotions and the graphic images she captures in her maiden collection can only be painted by a poet-observer who has lived the experience.

K. K. Bonteh

PART I
SNARL & SNIVEL

Hear My Broken Voice!

I can't be wrapped around like "miondo"
Nor be smoked like "mbonga"
I can't be pleated like a mud fish
Nor be tied up like a goat
I refuse to be beaten up like a snake
I refuse to be slaughtered like a fowl
I refuse to let them mow me down
I am me
They are they
We are us
I take them as "me"
Why do they always see a "they" in me?
Why are they squeezing my bones hard?
Why are they making me crawl?
Why do they want to extinct me?
What's the price to win?
Let them tell me
And I will give it to them even without working for it
Who owns the trophy?
Who holds the medals?
Who has the sticks?
Oh! Give me a snake beating!
Put red marks, brown marks or white marks
On my shiny black body!
Use your claws to staple my mouth!
Don't stop!
Smile!
Who's angry?
Who's bleeding?
Who's sweating?
Who's tired?
Storm my mouth with mud!
You'll always hear my broken voice!

Silence!

He came to our house
He arrested our hungry children
He cold-bloodedly killed our angry uncles
He shot our vibrant brothers in the marketplace
He raped our sisters out in the open
And pulled them into the mud
What did you do?

Silence!

He painted our walls with fresh blood
Even with dark clotted blood,
Clamped closed doors and windows,
Burnt mother's hut
Some spies burnt the old German schools
Behind our houses
The government schools, the police stations, the hospitals...
All disappeared like guilty ghosts at the appearance of fire
Our cousin, the one whose name was attributed a tag
Was accused of the act
The TRUTH, you knew
But what did you do?

Silence!

We talked of dialogue
My father went for dialogue
But trucks of guns made a triumphant entry into the compound,
Was it dialogue we wanted?

Silence!

Our children were frightened with guns
The same guns whose bullets rushed
Back to embrace their owners

Was it brother's faults that they fell?
Silence!

Wash your mouths with potable water
Wash your words with good reflection
You and a stick of match are not different
Don't blame anyone if there is a spark
Why are you complaining?
What did you expect?

Silence! Silence! Silence!

Silence can't solve our problem
Frank dialogue can throw some light
Mutual understanding can heal our wounds
Why are we silent on these?
Silence!

A Warrior's Torrent

I am caressed by the careless hands of fear
I am romanced by the rough fingers of hatred
My brother's blood is now cooking oil
My husband's body, chicken for supper
With waxen heart,
With sunken eyes,
With feeble legs,
With palsied mouth,
The scenes of the fierce spear of silence stabbing our screech
Open thorny red blinds before me,
When shall our subtle lips be opened?
I was brutally slapped by shackles,
Fear gave me another slap,
It shaved my desires
Yet boldness was the ligament that kept my bones intact with my flesh
Butcher me with your eyes,
Slaughter me with your words,
I shall kiss your weapons and take them to bed
I shall remove the man in them
And make them eunuchs
Your brutality shall impregnate me, and I shall give birth to warriors,
They'll vomit words that'll plaster your walls with peace
No matter how many stones you throw at me,
I shall walk bare-footed on the burning coal you put on my way,
Slap me! Rape my voice! Cover it under your iroko weight!
The arrow I possess is the orifice you'll be trapped in.

Tears of the Downtrodden

Africa cries,
I cry
Cameroon trembles and falls,
I cry.
I cry with my heart,
I cry with my lungs,
I cry, I cry,
I cry with my eyes open
Receiving the dust of time,
I cry with a broken heart,
A heart split by hatred, discrimination and isolation,
I carry the mark of the Mbororo bowls on my face
I walk with my cattle in the lonely streets,
I see pale faces of Mbororo children shining bleeding looks on
me,
Oh! How can I change the blood in their eyes into tears?
At least I can wipe tears,
For I see people shedding tears
Every second, every minute
Every hour, every day
Every week, every month
And even every year
Tears have flooded our streets,
Tears have taken our homes away,
Tears have swallowed our fathers, our mothers, our children,
We sleep in tears,
We swim in tears,
Swimming in blood will destroy us
But how are we to turn these tears into oceans of smile?

Children bleed in a country where thousands sleep in milky beds,
Did they ask to be born in a society where the word "poverty"
Is used as hashtag for their identification?
In a country where the stench of the cattle they rear
Is the axe used in splitting them from the rest of the world?

Like Salim said:

"I have been pushed to the borders of the society by people I call brothers,
People who look down on me and see nothing beyond my cattle rearing,
Nothing beyond the beautiful bowls I carry,
Nothing beyond my skin colour.
They call me names:
Invader!
Illegal immigrant!
Illiterate! (As if they gave me a school)
They put the word "Mbororo" on their lips and toyed with its pronunciation.

What can I tell my children?
How can I heal the wounds in their eyes?
Can I tell them that I had travelled across West Africa, Central Africa, North Africa,
To settle my legs on a soil that willingly wears a garment of poverty and exclusion on me?
My children, I am attacked by pests
These insects are pressing me down.

I walk with my cattle down the lane
I meet with long faces of Mbororo women
Fondling with a cell phone
An earnest desire for a selfie,
Quickly, a grudging thought speaks to me:
"Send me to school and not into marriage,
I can be the help you've been searching for long."
Certainly, my children, education is the key"

Oh, poor Salim!
In presenting your problem you create another problem - hate speech
It's a destroyer, the first spark to our problems
Though we bleed,
Though we cry,

We should cure our words first
Before curing the wounds.

Impregnated by Our Fathers

Our fathers have impregnated us
with illegitimate fantasies
Flashes of drunken hands
Staggering on fragile bodies!
Gutters of power
Pressing our backs on the ground,
Monsters, fuelling our wombs
with traumatized sperms
Oh! Who will suckle this neurotic child?

We've All Gone Mad!

Wolves, we see as toothless bulldogs,
Snakes, we take to bed with kisses,
We've gone mad!
We watch TV in a House on fire,
The smoke chokes us, our passion for the Series higher.
We cough, cry, yet refuse to look for water,
The neighbour is an enemy,
His hands, as good as water
To put out the fire

We've all gone mad!
Men, parading with foamy bras,
Boys, prancing with ladies' undies,
Kids, playing adults' games,
Girls, selling unripe apples to greedy hawks,
Wives, serving their husbands' food to unknown men in bigger
bowls,
We've gone mad! We're really mad.

We crack jokes and laugh on the corpses of our siblings,
We drink bottles of *afoh-afoh* and dance in the butchery
Letting our toes swim in thick clotted blood,
We feast with cups of blood at the butchery,
Spilling drops on our children's heads.
We're mad. We're really mad.

We mount tanks of scaffolds on moving carcasses,
Boneless fleshes,
Weary fleshes,
Fleshes divorced from gravity,
We mount their praises;
Cranky pale mouths bowing whitish lips
Like a flower in dire need of chlorophyll,
Strength, we release like scattered notes to produce a single note,
Boiling eyes,

Red spotted eyes,
Eyes infested by the dust from their footsteps,
Praises on lips,
Bruises in hearts,
Gifts in hands,
We are mad!
Truly, we're mad.

We're one mad people in a lost land,
Our madness has been ordained by our new gods,
We're wild cats dancing with fresh flesh,
We're stubborn cats humming and dancing in the heart of fire,
We're angels sparkling with vile minds,
We're lions with a tortoise's limbs,
We're mosquitoes with a rabbit's ears,
We're parrots resonating the master's words,
We're a generation of mad people
Playing cards with psychiatrists,
Our madness has been ordained by our new gods.

The Knock

(The Sound That Kills Many)

Knocking, knocking, knocking hard
Hard, hard, hard, it cracks the sound
Spilling echoes running mad
Mad, mad, mad, my dog is mad
Sharp teeth are quick to grind
Grind, grind, grind, my ear explodes
Oozing blood sings so high
High, high, high, the temper sighs
To the door like the dog flings so far
Far, far, far, to calm the pinch
It was the wind blowing fast
Fast, fast, fast, sighs and walks
Leaving hearts breathing hard
Hard, hard, hard, like my dog
To a shelter safety is sure
Sure, sure, sure, from the shouts
Oh, the sight of blood turning black!
Black, black, black, like their hearts
Where pretty flesh makes no sense
Sense, sense, sense, senseless hearts
Like the deeds they answered "Yes"
Yes, yes, yes, the years' command

Black Days

My days are darkened with fear
My future's windows are closed
One thing I hold so dear
My people have it priced
Who will pay this heavy price?
I litter the streets with doubts;
Will the struggle set a peaceful pace in my heart
Or rather with its ease make it uneasy?
I guess I must swallow my worries
But this unrest gives birth to many

Mary looks at me with a blink
At first when she did I felt my heart leap, for I knew all was bright
This heart of mine has been smashed, smashed, smashed and
smashed
By the unrest of the hours, it couldn't bulge when Mary blinked
It couldn't move when Mary, Sakwe, Epole, Agbor, Lum, Jean,
Kenyuy...
Sadly, and frightfully fled to the villages, like a rush hour
All were gone
Leaving behind echoes of their hearts' unrest
In empty classrooms did they cry, caught in the tricks of the yam
and the knife
In the hands of their beholder did their future lie

When will the price be paid? Everywhere I go there is blackout
But my father talks of the light of their time, his words illuminate
my senses
But mine, he says spread gloom. How won't they, when I live in
obscurity?
Those who had possession of the lamp failed to illuminate the
way
The holder of the yam and the knife should have the right deci-
sion to take

I know of Sundays; only did I fail to realise there was
A "Country Sunday", only the Bible's Sunday springs peace
My newly acquainted Sunday is uneasily pregnant
For we live in an uneasy peace, why not make the unrest rest
And give a golden chair for peace to sit on?
There are blackouts in our children's heads, in parents' hearts
breathe the pains
All broken hearts wish to be whole again

Mami Priscilla is tired of waiting, her business has no time to
waste
Into flames it rushes to taste the bitterness of the rioters' soft
hearts
How can rumbling stomachs be appeased, or pale mouths be
nourished
When all is gone in flames and my people's pockets sick and pale?
To the top all eyes are fixed, and hearts leaped with naked hope
so high
When broken hearts will be whole again, like the country's flag,
oneness shall prevail
Watch me dance as we ponder on the words;
"Together, we're one."

The Night

Dies Caniculares haunted all
Lambasted hearts sang dirges
As the pummel fell on us
Bodies, properties and hopes kaput,
Amortised to ashes,
They, the effigies of the state did these.
It was a pyromaniac night,
The air full of unheard messages
Suspended in the back of tongues
Of canicular sophistries,
Darkness stood before me in mini-skirt,
Soporific skirt,
And my eye lashes bowed
Though I sought asylum in this clawback skirt,
Stout claws still fell on me
Etching pains

A Hint to My Brother

O Brother!
Don't blame me if I didn't tell you the truth,
In fact, they sealed my mouth
Not only with Sellotape but with a masking tape.
I tried reaching out to you. Truly, I tried.
They clasped my neck with their arms
Prevented me from vomiting what was tickling me inside,
Forced me to scrawl on the piece of paper I sent to you.
O Brother! They tainted everything;
The message and our image.

O Brother!
If you only knew.
Their guns crowed in our ears,
We felt the soft touch of death
Gently taking us to the other side of the house;
Where our fathers are cooled by each drop of our blood,
Where tears wish to run down
But find reasons to be still.

O Brother!
If you only knew.
We crawled in our own house, the taps were flowing
But we were forced to bathe in the gutters behind the house.

O Brother!
If you only knew.
They butted in when we were about to call out to you
And bolted our doors and windows.
They buried our voices in our own house,
Making us shameful in front of our children
We didn't give up, Brother.
Yes! Brother, we didn't stop. We butted them out
In a way to pay tribute to the teachings of our Fathers,
Lest they blame us for neglecting their lessons.

O Brother!
We tried. Truly, we tried.
But they accused us of gabbling.
It will please our Fathers
And us, if you help us stand straight.

Hungry Voices

(The Silent Prayer)

O Mama!
Your eyes are now a river
To which we take our lovers
In it we hug and hover
Swelling our lungs and livers
Into Your warm breath we linger,

O Mama!
Your heart boils a boiler
Steaming the vapour higher
Into our eyes the sprayer
Digs deep the depth of water,

O Mama!
Your house is now on fire
Your children's bond on trier
Growing wild the flames of howlers
Suck'd hard the flat breast of anger,

O Mama!
Your children's voices wilder
To the sound of the howitzers
Pleating bodies and mind on hunkers
Flattery, corruption, killing walked glarer
Than the tear gas that gave a glimmer,

O Mama!
We know Your eyes are bleeding
Seeing their blood oozing
Oh! Our eyes are also bleeding
To see the union bruising,

O Mama!
We turn our eyes to You.
We put our knees before You.
We give our hearts to You.
Our tears and blood to You.
Our hope we give to You.
Our souls we bring before You.

My Last Wish

Take this cup away from me!
I tell you, take it away from me!
This, you gave me,
Surely you will enjoy having it,
I put it close to you.
I bring it back to you.
I give it all to you.
Take it! Not to leave it.
At your taste, see me no more.

Take this cup away from me!
I tell you take it away from me!
Your big bags won't crack my mind.
Brandish your big bags and speeches,
Flash tempting lights into my eyes,
Render moist my tympani,
At your taste, spelling blood;
The cup is filled to the brim
Take it now, it'll quench your taste.
At your call, see me no more.

Take this cup away from me!
I tell you, take it away from me!
The weight weighing down my frail hands,
Take it! Not to let it drop.
Not a print nor your shadow we want.
Not a foot to dance hard to stand,
Nor my people slip and fall,
To your taste the fall is sweet,
To our taste the fall is sour.
Take this cup away from me!
I tell you take it away from me!
We desire no such cup nor fall.
On mattress the fall is sweet,
On your floor we throw our spit.

Your eyes blink at its sight,
Take it and let us be!

Take this cup away from me!
I tell you, take it away from me!
The cup is more than me.
Your strength can carry it.
It's yours. Don't force it on me!
It presses me and presses my people.
Take it, and let us be!
Don't wait till all is gone,
To pick it up and take the road.

We Fear No Guns!

We fear no Guns!
Guns cooked this anthem and flag
We live with Guns
Their staccato is our alarm at dawn
And melodies for our sleep

We eat with Guns
Oh! The trembling of our pale lips
As we breathe their stringent fart every day long

We fear no Guns!

We fear no Guns!
Our brothers fondle them in bed
While our fathers fondle them like how they pluck our virginity

We eat Guns.
The mud we swallow in a basin of food stock in our mouths
We munch grenades and belch out war in our slums
Guns are castrating our peace

We fear no Guns!

Guns are our concubines
They give birth to children of war
Children reared in their cold bellies and poverty sadden shanties

We praise Guns
Guns of revolution that turned bitter,
Guns of freedom still born
We fear no Guns!

Guns, the rhythm and song of villages;
Guns, the other child of another
Guns, African infectious disease

Guns, the thunder that scares off peace
We are born warlords and war-ladies

We do not fear Guns!

Yaounde, 11 Nov 2017

Ashes

Yesterday's window flung widely open in my eyes
Like the large red skirt Solange wore
I paved through its tiny hole to grasp a glimpse
Of today's face
O! The smoke spelled tomorrow's
How am I to face a bleak day?
My eyes are covered with dust from the streets
My ears deafened by wailing sirens,
And hoots from khaki trucks scared all away
My legs are broken by their fists and boots
And my mouth stocked with their guns
O! Tomorrow spells ashes
Today we live with headaches
If only we could pause
To look at our faces in the mirror
Then we shall never call someone
"Animal"
For we are one in flesh and blood
But "if only" remains in my dreams
For the smoke has covered the mirrors.

Yaounde, 31 Jan 2018

Close Up!

War is shit!
Who honours war?
Hey you!
Do you?
Pack your luggage!
Follow wild animals!
Go sing to the bushes the honours of war!
Here, we piss on it!

Hey! Sama's eyes are closed.
Here they come to sing his praise.
Shit!
I piss on it!
Go wake up Zulu from his sleep!
Guess he'll tell you not to dare.
Common!!!
Don't feed my ears with that!
Go fight yourself,
If it be that honoured!
Send your children to the battle field!
Give them your guns, bombs or whatever!
If they fall, come forth and smile.
Shit!
War is rubbish!
I'll tell you why;
Who loves death?
Who enjoys tears?
Who likes digging holes
To bury loved ones?
I piss on it!
Come tell me war is sweet
I'll give you a close up.
Go bury your words in the king's pocket!

War is shit!
I spit on it!

The Ice Breaker

I'm fed up!
Give me your axe!
Oh no!
That can't help!
Give me your shovel!
Oh no!
It's as feminine as your spade.
Give me fire!
I think this may send me away.
I'm fed up!
Truly, I'm fed up!
Give me love!
This may inflate my heart.
Though fed up,
I don't need to be beaten by the wings of your love.
My heart is weighing down,
A mountain of ice is sitting on its seat,
Its shores are visited by ghastly figures,
It has been consumed by the ghoul,
Disfigured features girdle it,
I'm fed up!
I really am!
I need a break!
Give me an ice breaker!
This may scare them away,
It will melt that mountain of ice,
And my heart will sit up again,
To give light to its shores,
To enchant hearts of birds,
To give key notes to life,
I'm fed up!
Give me the ice breaker!
I need a break!
I need to break this ice.

Not Just News

I can feel the pains of their chains
Digging through my hungry flesh
I can feel their crocked hands
Pulling down my spinal cord
These pains are echoing
Scattered notes in my head
And I thought they were heard.
I can't take this anymore!
Not now!
Not today!
Not tomorrow!
I can't stand their rubbish sale!
Oh!!! I thought our people once bought themselves over
For I know of the blood our fathers shed
To the smile of our land.
If you should sit and watch
This nonsense act,
You're saying, "our fathers never fought for freedom,
That they crawled on their bellies to beg for freedom."
A freedom begged for
Is an empty freedom.
Look, they sit and watch the sale
Like dumbs in a choir.
They, whose eyes our Father gave to watch over us,
They, whose mouths are to speak for us,
They, whose hands are to protect us,
And now, look at them
Seated like imbeciles in their powers
To the gaze of the Libyan Act.
Oh! They are the same wolves
Toiling with our flesh,
The same wolves,
Tearing our flesh for food.
Snails have been enthroned
Where snails are Tigers

With a lion's roar
Let them use the roar to strike the Libyan Act.
Our people are sold in an era of freedom.
Oh!! Oh!!
Are we free?

Yet Another Song

I can hear their footsteps from a distant land
I can hear the rising tone of voices climbing up lifeless hills
It is the song.
It is the choir.
It is the national choir.
The choir masters and mistresses sing with hungry stomachs
I can feel the frightful trembling of their lips
From the disturbed notes that recorded the song
It is no new song;
The song they sing for the future had been sung over and over in
the past
It is a proud repetition of false notes,
It is a copy of an old song used to lure its listeners to sleep
It is the song I learnt at the age of two
It is the song I sing in the streets to free myself from stress
It is a national chorus
My ears are tired of listening to the same musical cords,
The same voices, the same messages,
It looks like newness has no business in recent politics
If they could change a black suit to a frog wear,
If they could grow their beards,
If they could spend one night in a bloody cold field,
If they could look deep into the eyes of a real street man,
They would understand why we need a new chorus
A new choir, a new chorister
A new rhythm, a refined rhyming pattern,
A new scenery to chant this new melody.
Oh! It is yet another song
My people still give applauses to it
As if they have a choice, as if they could beard a lion in his den

PART II
SLANG

Dogs Are Mad Again

Dogs have inhaled dried cold whisky;
Tots of power from poor master's cup
Have blown their brains;
Eyes ablaze with action,
Perception in confused directions,
Dogs have grown mad.
They rolled on the floor with treble barks
To act in stupor
At the scratch of poor master's
Commanding fingers,
A stun gun to stunt visions

Dogs have grown mad.
They're bringing down skirts of female preys
Tearing through their bushes with
Speedy limbs
In search of what could make them prey;
Dogs are chasing the wild
That danger to the master's seat
Hunting them to the very end;
Hard times, red eyes, dogs are mad.

Dogs are mosquitoes disturbing
Our peaceful sleep,
Creeping in darkness to waste our blood

Dogs are vampires toasting our blood
In closed doors
Beasts, slicing our bodies for honour rolls
Dogs are mad.
They're tossers tossing aside our movements
Stealing our rights in dark clauses,
Vultures feeding on their own carcasses
Dogs are mad again!

Pestiferous You

Who do these people think they are?
God?
Well, let me tell them they ain't God.
They can be something in the stale of their rooftops,
They can walk tall and reduce us with long eye lashes
They can make me lick the clitoris of their snakes
They can slap the hell out of me in their muddy parlours,
I'll wipe my tears and blame myself for being stupid
Stupid to believe gold existed in their sties
Stupid to have boarded a plane to be locked up in a cage
Stupid to frailly watch my siblings, from a distance, grow grey hair
and die
Stupid to sit and watch my tears playing hide-and-seek with me
Where laughter is a shadow that lives in the realm of my imagination

Are you the one time fellow whose love jumped from the heart
and fell on media pages?
Respect, you spell enticing us with your bait
Arrows at hand to stab our vigilance
Beasts in modern day's clothing
Sorcerers now live in mansions where hopes, dreams, tears, laughter and womanhood are buried.
If only we could bury yours in our bungalows
There, you'll see the devil live and understand that hell is far from
being abstract.

A Rainy Voice

The sky smiled, yet it rained on me,
The weather's face was bright,
When the harsh drops of rain
Clamped their palms on my face,
My jaws felt clammy

The drops fell on me like the obese world
They enveloped my body
And callously twirled my ear
With frozen fingers
Twisting it to have a kink,
A kink which made me a capon,
The slap of the drops of rain
Is a chisel on my chiselled body.

Oh, Mother! This letter I send
Is sealed with thick gum of tears that flow
From my sunken eyes
I send it under the heavy weight of the rain
If you find it wet, know it rains
Constantly on me.

Dance Now to Dance No More

If you like, dance.
Feel free. We're in a world with no chains.
Dance! Dance with the crown on your head;
Dance with your royal robe flying high;
Spread it on the royal seat
And move like an Ostrich sipping royal air;
Brandish your dancing style with pride,
Jump and dance!
Swing your royal legs on our fragile soils,
Crush our crops with your toes;
No! Swing them even further!
Spread them across borders;
Drop your hands like a kite
And hit us by surprise;
Carry them up, majestically, we shall kow-tow;
Dance! Dance! Dance!
When the drum shall sound,
You'll dance no more.

If you like, dance,
Dance with our huts on your head,
Dance with our loin round your groin,
Dance with our women in moonlight hotels,
Dance in your bathroom,
Pour our sweats on your smooth body,
Dance with our children's future in guarded malls,
Dance like a woman in hard labour,
Pull leaves from branches with your turbulent sound,
Use us like an Osier for your art;
Dance! Dance! Dance!
When the drum shall sound,
You'll dance no more.

The Wolves

Man, an animal in search of greener pastures
Tears through grasses, mindless of thorns
And with a wild soul wrapped in cold heart
Sharpens the teeth to crush any scrums on his way

Though he never was made a ferocious beast,
He puts on a wolf's clothing
Prancing, a king in the affair
Raping innocent souls with malicious acts
Ousting them from the sweet game of life
Chopping bodies of innocent children
Oh, logs they are, in the rough hands of butchers!
He pieces them into different sizes
Meat from the butchery
Cash crops exported to a land of no return
Where customers desperately wait in darkness

They've rubbed cold hearts in hot blood
Not blinking their eyes
Playing deaf in dead cries
Only the cries of hot cash they could hear
Tears of men their sweet wine is!
Weighing hard the size of their pockets
But never weighing hard the value of human life

I sing a song with a coarse voice
Flirting all my thoughts
With thoughts of men
Jammed by the absurdities of men
The loss of kids leaves no echo
Except the prolonged sorrow
In the fragile soul of helpless parents

If only drums could be played to wake up dead dogs,
    Oh, I'll hit my *bata* loud and clear; don't care

If birds fly away
For I seek to mend a rift in shattered spirits
I seek to heal a wound
Plucking leaves from barren trees
With the turbulent sound my *bata* plays
If only the trees could feel my touch ...

NNANE NTUBE & OLATUNBOSUN DAVID

The Chamber

A place of comfort
Where speeches saw delight in strolling,
Where hearts released all strings,
Where we sit as if in our parlours,
Has been robbed.
Thieves broke in and stole our comfort,
They took our legs away,
They buried our hearts in their eyes,
On our seats, they put thorns,
Compelling us to sit still,
Our words they use to pin us down,
Nothing can dare the almighty speaker,
His mouth, the mic of the chamber,
His words, our Bible be
Who dares?
The chamber has been robbed,
Thieves stole its name
The thieves we know but can't point out,
The thieves whose voices have overshadowed all TV stations,
The thieves who prance around like almighty devils
The chamber has been robbed of its seats
Its shadows have become numbed.

Cinch

Stop raining pity on me!
Love me.
Make me the roses of your bed.
Don't soak in tears
Each time I confess my sins
To bottles of beer!
By your strength,
I am who I am now.

Let my eyes speak to you
Let my tears touch you
Let my rocky body caress
Your stony heart
Our souls shall dine on the table of discourse
Where you and I will be victims of
One cause.

The Fall of the Baobab

(In memory of Morgan Tsvangirai)

I woke up with swollen eyes,
My ancestors had given me a black letter in my dream,
A dream I was alive to see,
Oh! In the letter I saw time sitting placidly on it,
Time had its careless hands in it,
The hands that once upon a time were soft,
It opened its wings and blew the wind
The wind was fierce, it came with spears
It pieced the feeble heart of the tree of reference,
I'm sure it missed its way,
It was a stray wind, my tree was its scape-goat
I saw it feeling uneasy after the strike,
It had lost its focus due to nature's call
I saw it folding its hands behind its back,
Pouring curses on those tiger stripes
Who gazed in dismay,
Who soon will serve their condolence in holey bowls
It promised them a sweet visit
And turned and wiped my tears;

The baobab fell, its fall was an axe put into my heart;
The sound it made can't be repeated by the sound of the drums
We'll play on the farewell day;
Time is furious for its mistake;
It kept the black letter in my hands and left
The baobab is gone, who will protect me?
Our inks are taking notes of its blessed memory.

The Baptism of Fire

Lord, you gave us your missal,
Taught us to pray with fire,
To chase the devil farther,
Oh Lord! We embraced the devil further,
Sealed a treaty of honour,
Graced by this honour,
We make our armour,
Your missal we used,
Yet, stroke with our missile,
Those who raised our legs higher,
We crushed them like crickets.
Oh, the pain was sweeter!
We saw in them our mourners.

We gathered in our glasses
To prepare for another outing,
For a start we needed your blessings,
You thought of a baptism,
Oh, the baptism of fire!
You came like thunder lightening,
Striking our glasses with your angry news,
Leaving the echoes of your rumblings
Into the desperate ears, they drop
Oh lightening!
Where will you land your next strike?

Wake Up!

My brothers! Who are you waiting for?
Why? Why do you look up to them?
Do you think they care?
See! See how they shake hands with them!
See how large their faces grow as they mingle dirty hands.
They open wide mouths and laugh at you.
And here you sit, waiting for their pity to drop like drops of rain.

My sisters! Why are you crying?
Oh! No! You've lost everything.
Well...
But what are you sitting here for?
Are you too waiting for Godot?
Listen! You better stand up straight!
Only you can trace your way.

My people, nobody cares!
See...you cry, and they feast.
Even if you lose everything,
Even if you bury them all,
Our people will still feast.
Ha! And you think the little box they gave you is a lovely gift?
It's an expression of their pity.
Get up from your hunger-stricken seat and work your way out!

Sweep the streets!
Wipe my wind-screen!
Roast fish by the beach! (That is, if you have one).
Bend down! Stand up! Walk!
Don't just sit. Unless you want to sell your name.
You! You! And You!
Go on! Go on and sell yourself!
We have seen sell-outs.
They've never changed their cloth.
Oh common! Go!

What are you standing there for?
Don't stick there like a rotten mango!
Go on! Be a wimp!
I repeat. Only you can trace your way.

Return —Not Going Further

I ran away from my father's land
Hoping to find peace—Yes, he did promise me
Peace and love—But where are they?
I ran away from my father's land
I ran hard and fast—I ran head hard—Heart drained
By its bleeding shore I slipped—it can't be the end of the road
I ran, I ran, on a hard stone I fell—Hard head—Hard heart
He didn't drop a tear seeing my bruising legs
Ah! I knew all was gone—the land —the peace —the love
It was a peaceful land (at least peaceful on pages—)
The peaceable land —at the time, had pissed me off —I doubt if I
took my heart with me
I didn't run for pleasure
I didn't run for leisure
I didn't run just to catch the sight of my lover —I don't think an-
other lover exists out there
My love hails from my father's land
My love had stayed behind
I ran with an empty heart —the farther, the emptier
I ran to a no-found love land
I left my father's land of peace and love —I was pissed off, —guess
I must return
Love is a hard nut to crack —let me crack it in my father's land
Peace is like a firefly rare to see —I'll use this torch and search for
it
Though the land bleeds and fades —I guess I'll still find my place
and face
My heart will be fat again
Oh! The milk and honey from my mother's chest!
My heart will be fat again
Oh! The palm oil in the boreholes behind our hut!
My heart will be fat again
Oh! The plum trees in our compound!
My heart will be fat again
Oh! The dry warmth of my people —My return will heal my bro-

ken heart
Faced with the broken walls of the land —peace and love have put
on a shadowy garment
My father's land is naked —Who will tie mother's loincloth round
its waist?

Close the gates!'
Close the doors!'
Close the windows!' —Only darkness can see our nakedness.
My escape has taught me a lesson —the neighbouring houses
were on fire,
Even smoke couldn't be seen.
'Return and close your outlets!'
'Take not the smoke any further!'

Yaounde, 1 Oct 2017 at 07:04

Where Shall My Abode Be?

I have seen on TV screens people crying and passing out
I read in a Newspaper (*Le Messager*) the dangers of such an act
I bought a bulk of it — On my walls I made my board;
Flirting memories did not shy away, on my bed I made a way
Where shall I go to? All is gone in flame and ash
Where shall my abode be? It rains heavily here
I took a walk down the lonely streets — Voices once heard, hurt
their stay and took a leave
Come with me, you'll see the scenes
Now deserted — a lift to goats and grasses
Am I alone to take this screenshot?
Where are those with beauty apparels?
My stay is due, my leave is soon
Hope to make it before the dune
As in my days seen no dew
I think there is need to make it two
For I have seen them moving in groups, a chain to paint their
state
And I; lurk alone — No strings to be attached to
Where shall my abode be?
In this lane, or that, or that?
Where shall my abode be? — Oh, I am lost!
I woke up from whencesoever I laid
The fidgeting thought dawned on me
The journals were right, they butchered their rights
Oh! I didn't take a ride!
My stay is sure. My placenta...buried in this shore
Where the land trembles with force
Though I saw many flaws and falls
The placenta will never sprout
There lies my abode — I was told.

If

I stood on a rough hill
Looking down the belle ville
Night spoke to me;
If you were the silence
Of this hour,
Wouldn't you enjoy your peace?

I blinked and looked clearer
Opening my eyes wider
I met Silence
But Peace was absent

Where was peace?
Was it lost in the dark corners
Of the belle ville?
Like in the beautiful streets of my mind?

Where was Peace?
Did it pull a black garment on itself?
The way life pulled a thick black garment on my thoughts?

Where was Peace?
Was it sleeping on the hips of night?
Like the way it slept in my memory?
Was peace lost amid light?

Even the night's silent breeze
Did not seem to have known Peace,
It visited me on my chilling hill
I thought I could find peace in its arms
It was just the same scaring figure that stood in front of my thoughts
Flattering me with shadows of reality
Making the muse news

If...if...
If only peace could reside in the tiniest ray of light,
If only silence could mean peace,
If only my mind could be decorated by the beautiful light of this belle ville,

I swallowed my "if" and buried my thoughts
In the darkness of the night,
A hope for an understanding,
A prayer for peace.

Amnesty's Request Is Tarnished

Walking like German shepherds
Landing on the Wouri shore
They saw the need to plant a seed
Like the wind, blowing the pollen
To fill the neighbours' eyes with dust
Steeping deep the roots with force
Till the war kicked them away
Division saw its roots
Decades and decades, it rests its arms
In illusion we saw oneness
Calling us for a shot
Begging us to sit round the peace plant
As the boilers boil their beans
Polluting the place with words that stink
Tarnishing amnesty's white request.

Awed by Silence

When silence frowns
The earth cracks
The dwellers tremble
The birds shriek with fear
Leaves cover their ears on branches
Branches bury their mouths in roots
Roots shamefully pull up failing eyes
Who is who in this state?

When silence coughs
Hearts beat
Mouths chillingly tremble
Legs sink to the ground
Eyes; as busy as bees
Who will take the blame?

When silence laughs
The sky cries
The atmosphere becomes alarming
Dwellers drink from cold hearts
And get drunk
Why not appease the dizzy soul?

Yaounde, 12 Feb 2018

Paving Through a New Dawn

We spread our leafy hands
To embrace a new dawn
The night's heat was sour
Where rested our unrest hearts
Heavy weight of tickling hours
Passed away like death;
Frustrated be
A new rise we seek
To sink through the bleak dawn
If we tie our hearts and hand,
We'll make smooth the tear
Without fear,
Without shedding tears;
And if we look behind,
We'll see we've reached the end
Of a new sunrise
The brown new dark door
Certainly, will not darken our hearts
With fear
To see our legs shying away

Life-Blood

(The Message)

The year has finally died away
And here I am sitting and wondering,
When will I hear this angelic sweet sound:
"School is a good thing, learning is a good thing..."
When will I hear these words that usually hang in the air like fog?
Maybe all are asleep
No! No! No! No! They can't be!
If all were asleep, snores would have given reason for that.
I wonder where they are.
I woke up from my dream and decided to search for them,
Those whose eyes are red and mouths, tasty for change.
In the shattered and lifeless streets of towns, I searched and
searched and searched
In lifeless markets of towns where books and bags are veiled,
I searched and searched and searched.
In schools where the voice of the voiceless resides, I searched and
searched and searched.
Till I met a dead cold whose chilly embrace stole a smile from my
face.
I felt delighted as I roamed with my shadow in these ghost towns.
Where else could I search?
Is it in churches where youths find delight sitting outside,
Chatting with friends they couldn't see within the week
Or those they saw yet have a lot to say?
Is it in bars where parents show no difference from youths?
Is it in night clubs where darkness reigns and movements pattern
by heavy deafening sounds?
Is it in the East where nothing is done,
Youths and parents bury square heads into rectangular phones,
Laptops or other social media gadgets?
They exhaust themselves with worthless thoughts and leave be-
hind what's important to do.

I'm tired of searching. Tomorrow I'll search again.
Tell them I searched. Maybe your words will give meaning to the course.
Tell them their brothers are anxiously waiting in the nearby caves and bushes
For a positive reply.
Tell them we seek to hear the harmonious melody again.
This time refined and promising.
Maybe they will leave behind their fears and give meaning to this innocent song.
Tell them the future awaits us at the next door.
If not, this recommended course will be as silent as a graveyard
If not, our country's fate will sleep in old hands where dormant decisions are made
Where conferences are attended by tired and sleepy leaders
Where a "yes!" is given to give delight to a brother and not to nation building.
There is much to do. We need to act promptly and efficiently.
We should say adieu to the old, weary and decaying foundations.
I'll not stop till I search and find the hand that can break all the old stones.

August 2017

The Dreadful Path

Silence gave its name,
Cold by the dry windy cool
Invisible creatures spread invisible footsteps
Quick! A cat passes by,
Tearing hearts apart like the world map
Stillness hangs in the air like a cloud covering my eyes
Voices of the unknown make hasty noise
Pushed by dry windy cold
Fleshy hearts strive to be silent
Lest they break the silence of their voices
And the bleak falls on them
Swallowed by the bleakness they dread,
They retreat with heavy legs
Who can dare the shadow that stands?
Even the mighty courage shies away
From the shadow of the hearts' rest
Though unrest in the world beyond
Now it stretches to our world
At the death of the hour
Where black cats, stray dogs and owls
Celebrate the dawn of their day
With music tuned from nightingales
Dances varied from nocturnes
But hearts are still in the face of gloom
At the sound of the dead hour
Dead creatures make their way
To the path we dread to cross
Oh, the shadow that we face!

Black Worries

Oh sleep! Sleep!
Let me sleep on a bamboo bed,
As if I have a choice.

Oh eat! Eat!
Let me eat your leftovers,
As if I have a choice.

Oh dance! Dance!
Let me dance while you eat,
As if I have a choice.

Oh stand! Stand!
Let me stand with napkins ready while you eat,
As if I have a choice.

Oh quiet! Quiet!
Let me quietly sit while you infest my eardrums with insults,
As if I have a choice.

Oh silence! Silence!
Let me be silent while you chop my bones into pieces,
As if I have a choice.

Oh retreat! Retreat!
Let me retreat while you sun your bullets on me,
As if I have a choice.

Oh praise! Praise!
Let me sing your broken praises,
As if I have a choice.

Oh follow! Follow!
Let me follow you like a shadow,
As if I have a choice.

Oh listen! Listen!
Let me keenly listen to your lies without a word to defend myself,
As if I have a choice.

Oh tell me! Tell me! Tell me!
Do I really have a choice?

Litany of A Foreign Wife

I love it when you call me
"Honey" or better still "my better half",
But hate it when you call me
"This woman" or worst still, "my Engled wife",
You claim to build a bridge,
Yet you broke the ridge
On your refusal to see me climb up to your reach.

My husband, treat me fairly
Don't caress me as you wish
Or when your quest for exploration is at its peaks
And tomorrow spit on me
When I, a wolf, seek for food
In a union that swept my rights away,
A union with no communion,
A union where no tables were properly dressed
Nor I, properly addressed

You picked up your chewing stick
And brushed your brown teeth,
Spitting out all sorts of germs
Which infected my toes and fingers like hungry jiggers
Then to your pleasure, you gave me your images:
"Dog", "zombie", "zozo", "fool", "terrorist woman"
My husband, did you really love me?
Let's face ourselves and say the truth
Else my "things" will cross the line
Which I think never existed
Did you really love me?
Were you enticed by my mountainous shape?
Were you captivated by my fertility and fidelity?
Was your sole desire to run the race that many once ran?
Or, was it to run the race where many watered throats to run?

I love you, I love our children and I love myself
No need to make me now your other woman,
I cease to be your African woman
When you put on your cheating cap,
When you firmly hold your phallic stick,
Treating me like your servant,
I cease to be your African woman
When the stinking calabash you hold is a trumpet in my head.
Time whispers to me. Yes! It did.
I must stand up!
Else I'll remain your humble shadow

My husband, treat me fairly,
Drop your hate speeches in the dustbin
And reflect on how our future should be,
I'll be glad to have you back
If only you give me my rightful place
And let me savour my own beauty
Then, I'll humbly be your African pearl.

ACKNOWLEDGEMENTS

I would like to extend my heartfelt gratitude to Professor Ba'bila Mutia for his relentless encouragement, guidance, and for proofreading this work. My appreciation equally goes to Mr K.K. Bonteh for accepting to review this work within a short period of time, and to Nsah Mala for his encouragement and edits. I would love to acknowledge Spillwords Press, New Ink Review, Atunis Galaktika Online Magazine, Bravearts Africa and Tuck Magazine for publishing some of the poems in this work for the first time.

ABOUT THE AUTHOR

Nnane Ntube is an award-winning poet whose poems have been performed widely across Cameroon. She is a youth leader, mentor, volunteer, performer and Youth Envoy for Peace and Democracy. Her poems have been featured in leading magazines and online platforms such as *Spillwords Press, Tuck Magazine, Writers Space Africa, Tushstories, Bravearts Magazine* and in anthologies such as *Best New African Poets 2018, Medley of Melodies, Influence of Indian Classics on World Literature, Break the Silence, Ashes and Memories, The Gifted Pen* and many others. Nnane holds a BA in English Language and Bilingual Studies (French and English) from the University of Yaounde 1 and currently pursuing graduate studies in the department of African Literature and Civilization at the same institution. She also holds additional diplomas in teaching from the Higher Teachers' Training College of the University of Yaounde 1. Nnane teaches French and English at the Government Bilingual High School, Bafia.

Printed in the United States
by Baker & Taylor Publisher Services